The

Overseas

Basketball

Blueprint

A Guidebook On Starting And
Furthering Your Professional
Basketball Career Abroad For
American-Born Players

Dre 'DreAllDay' Baldwin

Introduction

Since I started my website <u>DreAllDay.com</u>, along with all the <u>YouTube videos</u>, I have received many requests from players on playing pro basketball. And since the NBA has only so many positions, most of you know that overseas ball is a stronger possibility for you to continue your playing career, and it is: The NBA has 450 job positions while there are 10,000 players employed internationally (which includes Canada, Central and South America, which technically do not require going "over a sea" to get to, in case you cared).

Over the years I have compiled several guides and tips for players on how to get their careers started, what to expect on the way and once they are in the door, and how to handle themselves with the on and off-court situations that come with it. Every guide comes from questions that players frequently ask me.

This guidebook is a compilation of all of those guides and tips in one place for your quick and easy reference, which I will be updating over time as new questions come up and new information arises. It should be noted that several, though not all, of the chapters of this book are based on the posts on the Guides & Tips page of my website, edited and updated for this guidebook — so do not leave me any negative reviews saying, *"It's just the same stuff from his website!"* I'm saying here and now that many things are the same, but there is also new stuff in here, and everything is updated to fit the times. And it's damn two-ninety-nine. Quit your whinin', make the pros, write a book about it and sell one copy — you've made your money back!

If you take only one thing from this guidebook, know that professional basketball is a buyer's market: There are more candidates than there are jobs, so the people who do the hiring — the teams themselves — have the power. What this means for you is, you need to make yourself stand out. Make these coaches, agents, and managers remember you and want to know more. We will cover this within.

Let's get started.

The Basics: What You Need to Know to Have A Pro Basketball Career

Being that I came from a small college background and never played a second of AAU ball or was ever offered a scholarship, I receive many inquiries from players in similar situations as to how they can get their foot in the door of the pros. What follows is a sketch of what, in my opinion, is most important for such individuals to get into the professional ranks. If you agree and/or think this list can/will/did help you, great! Don't even waste time telling me — get to work. If you disagree with my list, I don't care.

1. Make A Fucking Decision.

"A real decision is measured by the fact that you've taken a new action. If there's no action, you haven't truly decided." – Tony Robbins

I decided sometime late in my college years that I would be playing basketball after I graduated. I was 100% committed, even though I had no idea how or where or when I'd get there. There was no Plan B. A player who sits the bench at Duke or Michigan State for four years will get professional offers from teams just based on the fact that he/she was on the roster at one of those schools, without even expressing interest in playing professionally. Some of them can actually play, and some can't — I have seen this with my own eyes. Some of those players take those offers, and some don't.

My point, however, is that a player with a 'D3' or 'NAIA' or whatever else there is out there on their resume will have to go and create their own opportunities to get a contract. I know many players from small schools who *say* they wanna play overseas, but their commitment is one of convenience. Meaning, if it is made easy enough for them, enough doors are left unlocked and cracked open, they'll put in the necessary effort. When the going gets tough, their careers end quietly, and, as Porky Pigs says, 'that's all folks!'

I had to knock down doors, and in many cases, build my own, to get where I'm at. And I'm still building doors to this day. And, as that Tony Robbins quote says, the true mark of your decision is when you start taking some action. Sending someone (like me) and email saying, "I want to play overseas, can you give me some information?" is NOT taking action. Asking someone to tell you what to do is not an action step. Real action involves the other steps you learn as you read further...

2. You Need Film.

If you played in college, collect film of every game you played in that you can get. Nowadays, most schools film their games — get the film ASAP. You never know what may happen. You transfer, fall out with the coaching staff, coach gets canned... Make an ally in the athletic department and get your film.

The person in charge of the video is usually very accessible. Don't make a big deal about getting your film — coaches can get antsy about a player wanting his film in the middle of the season — quietly collect those tapes/ DVDs/video files and keep them in a safe place (Google Drive and Dropbox are more reliable than the hard drive on your laptop which can be lost, damaged or stolen). Never let the originals out of your sight. Make copies.

Film is your job interview to pro teams — if they haven't seen you play in person, and you have no film, your only recourse is to attend an exposure camp — for which you pay for travel, hotel, food and possibly exorbitant camp entry fees (not to say that a camp could not be a great investment). When I was graduating college in 2004, my school recorded some games, but not all of them. My sophomore year coach had all the 2001-2002 games on film — but he had given the originals away to players when he lost his coaching job. I went online and found contact numbers for the teams I had played against my last 2 years, and offered to mail self-addressed stamped envelopes to each them to get copies of game film. It's *that* important. If you do go to an exposure camp, any one worth its cost offers film now (we will get to that in detail), either streaming online, downloadable, or for purchase via DVD. Whichever format you prefer, get it and keep it.

3. Work On Your Fucking Game.

The simplest of all these bullet points. Practice. Train. Improve. Get better. I have stressed this over and over on YouTube to the point that you have probably heard me same that statement before in a video, multiple times. Think about Michael Jordan. He is arguably the best basketball player in the history of the universe. Even at the height of his greatness (the entire 1990s), MJ worked on his game. And he was better than me, you, and the person next to you. So if the best player in the world was still working on his game when he was at the top of the mountain, what makes you or anyone else think they don't need to put the work in to improve? Don't answer that.

4. Show Your Game.

A lot of players come to me with their highlight films, as if I am a scout, asking for "contacts" — when the people to whom you need to be showing your video are the agents and coaches and managers. Having skills in basketball and not being seen is like having a bunch of money in cash locked in your attic or basement. Yes, you are rich, but the power of money is in its use and circulation, not the act of possessing it.

I'm not telling you that you have to play in every league or game that takes place. But if you are a good player, you want people to *know that*, right? Then show up where the other good players are and show 'em what you've got. Ask around for where the best players are — anyone who lives in a town that plays basketball at all knows where the best games are, whether they themselves play there or if they know better than to embarrass themselves trying. Point is, they know. Soccer players know where other guys play soccer. Lawyers know which bar other legal workers go to get drinks. Basketball players know where the tough games are taking place.

5. Network.

Sounds simple, but many players don't do it. There are millions of people in the world who want to play basketball for money; not all of them will. You are not the only one. Ask around — your local gym; coaches you know; players in your weekly pickup games — there's always somebody who knows somebody. Trust me. If you're a male, female friends know other guys who play ball. Find out where good players work out or where they play pickup or what leagues they play in during the summers. Diffidence or arrogance when it comes to approaching others won't help you here — the simplest way to make a new friend is a smile and a "hello."

6. Nobody Owes You A Thing. Including me.

When it is all over, whatever you accomplish (or don't accomplish) is credited 100% to you. Not your college coaches, not your girlfriend or teammates, not your agent. No matter what anyone else does or doesn't do for you, promises and doesn't come through on, 'hates on' you, it's your life and career.

I once heard a smart businessperson rhetorically ask, "What's your IQ?" He wasn't referring to intelligence — this IQ stands for "*I Quit.*" What has to happen for you to give up? How far will you go? How much can you take? If you reach out to someone for help and they decline to help you or let you down, is that your excuse for giving up? If you want to make it, you will. If you want to find an excuse, you will. If you need help, start by looking in the mirror. Ask yourself what you'll do if (and when) no one helps you.

How Overseas Basketball Works: A Guide

Every time I meet a person and they ask me what I do, this happens:

"I play basketball."
"Oh! For who?"

What follows is some answer about playing overseas or a certain country or the last place I was at. If I'm lucky, the question-asker is satisfied and the conversation ends. Other times they are not satisfied, and the conversation doesn't...end... there.

"How does that work?"
"Do you play against other countries or...?"
"What league is that?"
"Is it better than the NBA or...?"
"So, why don't you play in the NBA? Have you ever thought about it?

I am sure a lot of players can relate to this exchange and the 15-minute explanation that follows.

This guide will explain, for the uninitiated — be it for players, or fans of basketball — how things work, in a general sense.

Every Country Has Its Own League Within the Country, Just Like The USA Has The NBA.

A player who "plays in Italy" plays for a team in an Italian league, against other Italian-based teams in that Italian league. The team travels throughout Italy, playing road games against those teams. The rival teams also travel to the player's home town, to play at their building. Just like the New York Knicks travel to Boston, Los Angeles and Denver for games, and those cities' teams travel to NYC to play the Knicks. Simple.

Unlike The NBA, International Basketball Has No Player's Union (For Protecting Players) Or Salary Requirements (For Protecting Teams), So **How Much Money A Player Makes Is A Wide-Open Situation. Very Wide-Open.**

The NBA has minimum and maximum salaries because of the NBPA (National Basketball Players'

Union), which protects players' rights, and the CBA (Collective Bargaining Agreement), which is a contract between all NBA team owners and the NBPA.

The NBPA, in basic terms, fights for certain minimums for players (your own hotel room on road trips, a certain amount of per diem money, a league-wide minimum salary, etc) and goes to bat for players when there are player-ownership disputes (fines, suspensions, etc).

The CBA is created for the owners (the NBA as a business, is essentially all 30 owners — the commissioner works for the owners) to protect themselves against the NBPA — maximum salaries (which did not always exist), dress codes, suspension guidelines, fine penalty regulations, guidelines on what can and cannot constitute "late" to practice, etc.

The NBA is the only basketball league in the world with a players union. This means, if you play in any league other than the NBA, you have no one looking out for your rights, save for your agent (if you have one). You are on your own. I have seen players sign multi-year deals for millions, and I have seen players who play for no pay. Americans overseas, in general, always are afforded a place to stay (not necessarily a *nice* place, but a place), and some amount of food — again, this runs the gamut from every single meal paid for and/or prepared, to you being on your own in eating. All of these things can be negotiated in your contract, based on your negotiating position and power to even negotiate in the first place (which many overseas players lack).

Overseas basketball is a buyer's market: There are more available players than there are available contracts, so teams can be picky and make take-it-or-leave-it offers to players, who, often, take such offers for fear of being left with nothing, which in turn drives salary down for all of us.

There Are A Few Select Top-Level International Teams Who, In Addition To Their Domestic Leagues, Play In A Group Against Each Other. This Is Called The "Euroleague".

Unless you personally know a person who plays overseas, this is probably the only International basketball you have heard of. The Euroleague is the best league in the world outside of the NBA. It consists of 24 teams, from various countries, who are considered the best of the best (Note: in Europe, many times one club can "leapfrog" another in terms of leagues and levels not by way of team performance on the court, but by buying their way in. This happens at the domestic and Euroleague level. So the Euroleague is not necessarily the "best" 24 teams in Europe, but they are a good, close representation).

Many very good current NBA players have played in the Euroleague; Manu Ginobili is one such player. If you are a college basketball fan and one of your favorite school's top players didn't quite make the NBA (or he did, but didn't last long), there is a good chance he plays for a team that competes in the Euroleague. Keith Langford, Shelden Williams, Sean May, Drew Neitzel, Joey Dorsey, Josh Powell, Hilton Armstrong, Acie Law, Nick Caner-Medley, Matt Walsh, Omar Cook and Bracey Wright are just a few such players who are or have been in the Euroleague at some point in their careers.

Not Speaking The Native Language, For Americans, Is Not Much Of An Issue As Most "Young" People (30-Under) Speak English.

I only speak English (and some Spanish) and have never had an issue getting around in any place I've been. Students in non-USA take English classes in school and watch tons of American TV; they know the language well, and a lot more about our culture than you'd think.

The older people, I've seen, are the ones who don't speak English many times and don't care to learn (I have had multiple non-English-speaking coaches; that has been fun). But with a combination of basic English, a pocket translator (or phone app) and some gesturing (which is how I purchased condoms in Kaunas, Lithuania), you'll get by.

Playing In Europe (Or Any Other Continent) Is Not Necessarily A "Better" Way To Get To The NBA. It Is Not Necessarily Worse Either.
&
The NBA's D-League Is The Closest A Player Can Be To The NBA Without Actually Being In

The NBA. But Many Good Players Don't Play There. There Are Good Reasons Why.

The NBA is the most popular basketball league in the world, it has the best players, facilities, living/ travel situations, and offers the most money.

But there are only 450 jobs in the NBA.

What this means: There are many very good basketball players who simply cannot *all* play in the NBA at the same time.

European clubs and NBA teams respect each other's contractual agreements, which means this: Say you sign a contract with a team in Spain and play well, averaging 30 points per game for the first month of the season. The Chicago Bulls notice and want to sign you. They cannot act on this urge, however, until after your Spanish season is over, because you are in a binding contract with that Spanish team until the season is over or until/if that team decides to let you out of it early (highly unlikely, especially if you are playing well). So, signing with an overseas team is a season-long decision for players, forgoing a chance at the NBA that season (presumably, since the contract usually lasts well into the corresponding NBA season) when they sign that deal. Play well that season, and that player may get an NBA opportunity the following season.

The other option is the D-League, the NBA's official minor league. The D-League does not offer much by way of compensation — their salary range is published online in many places — and houses you college-student style with the rest of the team. The level of play is high, the lifestyle is anything but. 15-passenger vans, Wal-Mart food trips and coach-class flights are part of the D-League existence (which I don't completely get, since the NBA backs the D-League the same way they backed the WNBA for many years before the WNBA was turning a profit. WNBA players play and practice in the same facilities as the NBA teams many of them share cities with, and earn 3-4X more money than D-Leagers).

BUT, in the D-League, say you have that same great 30-point-per-game month that Hypothetical You had in Spain. In this case, an NBA team can sign you immediately; you could be playing for the

San Antonio Spurs the very next day. You can go to (i.e., be called up by) an NBA team at any time when you are a D-League player, as opposed to being contractually married for a year or more (based on your contract) to a team overseas. By playing in the D-League, you are essentially betting on yourself in the chance that you'll be one to hit that NBA contract lottery (which would be pro-rated for the amount of time you actually spend with a team). You can be called up and sent down between the NBA and D-League the same way baseball teams do their minor league players, with certain restrictions for teams in terms of frequency, player experience, etc.

So, many players have to choose between a year-long commitment to an overseas club, who could offer a better living situation, more money, and long-term stability on and off the court, and the chance of winning that lottery of being called to an NBA club in the D-League.

This is not an easy choice as basketball players are people just like you; we want to live comfortably and have responsibilities — families, kids — outside of simply satisfying our basketball desires. We have to consider the endgame of basketball, hopefully putting ourselves in a position to continue living comfortably when our careers are done.Thusly, many really good players choose to play out their careers overseas, even when they have NBA teams wanting them to come over for non-guaranteed opportunities.

30 teams. 15 roster spots, up to 450 players total. Approx 85 players that were on rosters in 2012 were out of league in 2013. #NBA
— JALEN ROSE (@JalenRose) July 9, 2013 via Twitter

Let's get into exactly what that means.

NBA Training Camps are basically tryouts in the NBA — for example, the Miami Heat will have 20 or so guys in Camp, but only 15 make the team. Guaranteed contracts — contracts the team has already agreed to with certain players — play a role in who makes a club also (some teams go into Training Camp with 15 guaranteed players already signed, but as a player, you may still take the Camp invite just to get the exposure and "NBA Training Camp" on your resume). Unlike in the NFL, every cent agreed to in an NBA contract is guaranteed, no matter your performance.

Say, you just played a great season in the Euroleague and decide to give the NBA a shot the following season. The best overseas offers usually are offered in the summer. NBA Training Camps begin in October. So to take this shot, you are giving up your chance at the best Euro offers that year, which will be long gone by October. But the NBA is your dream, so you go for it. You outplay an incumbent player who was on the team the previous year — but that guy's contract is already guaranteed for the upcoming season. So the team you're in camp with — which, remember, is also a business — decides to pay just one guy (the guaranteed-salary player whom you outplayed) instead of paying two player (you, and the incumbent they had to cut to sign you — remember, that contract is guaranteed; he gets paid even if he doesn't play).

This is the "numbers game" you hear of often when players get cut from NBA teams. You miss out on the NBA and now the best overseas offers are gone, taken by players who decided in the summer that they weren't going after an NBA roster spot.

This is the craps game that overseas players opt out of to have a more steady situation basketball and money-wise abroad. Again remember, athletes are people with lives to live. Everything must be considered.

Overseas Basketball Players Have A Ton Of Free Time On Their Hands. There Is A Wide Range Of What Is Done With That Time.

Just like you, I roll my eyes when I see a basketball player release a mixtape or upload a freestyle to YouTube. But I completely understand. As basketball players overseas, you're looking at a max of 5 hours per day of actual "work" time, and the rest is up to you. You must find something to do.

Some make rap music or sing R&B. I write blog posts, make videos and read books. Some chase entertainment in bars, nightclubs and females. Some play video games. Some draw or paint. There is enough time to take up a serious hobby when playing basketball is your job. So when you see a ball player doing one of the aforementioned things, it doesn't mean he's not dedicated to the game or his team (also doesn't mean he *is*, but that's another post for another time).

How To Acquire An Agent For Overseas/Professional Basketball

If you are seeking an agent to help get you a job playing professional basketball, understand this: An agent is only as good as you are. Meaning, no matter how great of a salesperson your agent is, if your game video shows an inadequate player, there isn't much your agent can do with it to get you signed. An even if he does pull off a magic trick and gets a weak player signed, you can't hide behind your agent on the practice/game court. The team will see what you are or are not, and that will be that.

What Agents Do For Your Playing Prospects

As far as overseas ball goes, agents = connections. An agent knows people whom you don't know, and can have relationships with clubs where a particular club will trust that agent's word on players (whom the agent represents) to sign next.

This helps both sides: the team saves time searching databases of literally thousands of players who want to play pro ball, and the agent gets his clients signed and paid (and the agent gets paid — by the team, NEVER by you). Of course, it's important that the agent be good to his word, meaning that the players he sends to a team better be good players. If an agent sends a weak player or two to a team the agent has built a relationship with, that team may decide to "turn off the faucet," so to speak, with said agent and take their talent search elsewhere.

So an agent is incentivized to have a stable of good players to send around the world. Meaning, when an agent turns you down or ignores your request for representation, that's their way of telling you they don't feel they can a) market you properly and/or b) get you singed and/or c) keep their good name by sending *you* to a team they have a relationship with. Some agents may say that they have too many clients at the time to take on more, which may be true. But if LeBron James walks into their office with the same offer, he's leaving with a new agent. Take that for what it's worth.

As far as exposure goes, agents can get you into camps or combines where you can be seen by overseas decision makers, sometimes covering entry and travel fees on your behalf (which the agent expects to make back by you getting signed to a contract in the future — nobody does something for nothing). An agent could also get you included in invite-only workouts or tryouts that you wouldn't be able to talk your way into alone.

Many agents I've dealt with work on non-exclusive agreements — which means that they represent you on a case-by-case (or contract-by-contract) basis, and if they get you a contract, they get paid (by the club) for bringing you to the club and they'll take the credit for getting you signed (usually in the form of posting you/your good news on their website, Facebook page etc. as credibility for their company — sometimes they take credit even if they *didn't* get you the deal!

But no real harm in this; it just puts your name out there in more places (which can't be bad). But, if during the course of waiting on a contract, Agent B or some other opportunity arises for you, you are 100% free to take advantage of that other situation with no legal recourse by your non-exclusive agent. This works for both sides: the non-exclusive agent doesn't feel the weight of you waiting and depending fully on them, and you are free to pursue deals on your own or with any other non-exclusive agents out there.

Most agents will be clear about this situation up front: *"We will work on getting you a job, but you're free to look on your own too. If you do take a contract elsewhere or with another agent, just tell us, so we aren't promoting you for jobs you are not even available to take."*

Some agents/agencies, however, will want players signed to them exclusively. In my experience, this happens with higher-level players (read: you came from a bigger college) or players who have proven themselves very well in a particular job/country, so the agent pretty much *knows* he can get you another contract, thus he wants full rights to you. This works great for the agent for obvious reasons, and also for the player, who can relax knowing that his agent is doing all the marketing and sales work for his next contract; all the player has to do is be in the gym practicing, in game shape, and be ready to go when the call comes. The best-paid players I've known have all been in exclusive agreements with their agents. Exclusive agreement = a signed, binding contract between you and an agent.

So what if you have no agent, what can you do? You can reach out to agents. Eurobasket is a good resource for agencies (there's an Agents page with links/info to a bunch of agencies). You can also do simple Google searches for agents in your area (maybe you can meet someone face-to-face or have them see you play if you have no stats/video).

What do you say to them when you do reach out? Sell yourself! Why should that agent give a damn about you, what with the hundred other emails/calls he's getting from random hungry players? This is your job to do — figure out what makes you worth the time and express that. Always remember: talk is cheap. Saying you're hungry and telling some person who has never heard of you how good of a shooter you are and what your vertical is means *less than nothing*. Offer to send a video over and/or some stats from your last playing situation (better yet, include it in your initial contacting of them). Don't have any video or playing situations? Get off the internet and go get some. If you are not good at this sales thing, work on it and learn: Sales skills will help you in all areas of life, well after basketball (whenever that is).

——

Your other option, sans agent, is to market yourself directly to teams (again, Eurobasket). This is how I built 90% of my playing career, though times have changed from when I graduated college in 2004. How so? There are many more players out there (there were plenty of players then, too, but we seemed more spread out since the internet was not so big — I sent a VHS tape to my first agent, for example), many more exposure camps (there were only about 5-10 total, all summer, back then — now there are 100), everyone is online sending emails and YouTube links, so there's generally more "noise" for agents to cut through.

Bottom line is, you're looking to play professional sports, which means you are claiming yourself to be an adult. I did not write this as a color-by-numbers guaranteed way for you to get on (and I am not an agent myself, nor do I have a pipeline to any for you). You're a man/woman: Be one and take responsibility. Be creative and do what you have to do, so later on you can do what you wanna do.

Good luck.

1. Market myself to Agents via email using stats from last time playing: Gotham Hoops

2. Send the same stuff directly to Pro teams

3. Play in leagues and accumulate/keep track of stats - also film those games.

4. Find team GM's and coaches and send my stuff to them!

I Don't Know Where to Begin... Help!!!

I hate that I am actually having to write this. And I'll tell you why:

Most of you are not cut out for doing this (basketball) as a profession.

And I'll tell you why that is, too. Based on the emails and comments and messages I have received over the last 6 years of having this website, the majority of people I hear from want a few things, in no particular order:

- A guaranteed, safe way of continuing their basketball lives
- A step-by-step guide on making it, that is basic color-by-numbers "do this, then this, then that" directions — like using the Maps App on your mobile device
- To believe that, other than what I have already shared, that there just might be some other information on getting there that I'm withholding *just for you*, and if you email/comment me I'll reveal the missing secret.

I will say this here, for those of you who don't read (and that's a lot of people): This business is for hustlers.

What do I mean when I say this business is for hustlers? What's a hustler? What does a hustler do?

- A hustler begins, sometimes knowing nothing about how or when or where or who. They fix things along the way.
- A hustler never stops moving.
- A hustler improvises and does what (s)he needs to do when the situation calls for it.
- A hustler figures out what to do, on their own volition, when there are no instructions to follow.
- A hustler creates something out of nothing.
- A hustler thrives when there are no rules.

Playing pro ball from a small, unknown school? From being in school but not on the team? From no school whatsoever? It's not about your crossover or the backspin on your jumpshot or what position you prefer playing. When you come from/go to a small school (basically, anything that is *not* an NCAA D1 or very high D2), hustling creates your career, and anything basketball-related that follows. Physical talent and skill alone won't suffice.

Your mindset is the key here. A hustling mindset knows that nothing is handed out and you have to *make a way*. Do you understand what *make a way* means? It means that no one can tell you exactly what to do or "show (you) the way" — if it were that simple, everyone would be playing, and that person who showed you could write a how-to book and sell it for a nice, easy profit. There are no rules in the business — and even when rules exist, they are obeyed when people *feel like* obeying them. Your situation is yours only — no one has your exact circumstances and you shouldn't put anyone else in the position of asking them to decide "what (you) should do". If you're looking to play college or pro ball, that means you're and adult or damn close to it — act like one. Own it.

Basketball careers are not your normal 9-to-5. It is not like school, where everything is laid out ahead of time, everyone has the same goal and benchmarks, and you can always blame the teacher's lack of helping you when you fail. There is no one to depend on when you fuck up or get fucked up, like being a child living at home with your parents. You can get fucked over by this person or another, and there is no (useful) legal recourse in many cases. Getting one (job, scholarship, roster spot) means nothing as far as the next one is concerned in many cases; you never stop hustling.

So you don't know where to begin, huh? I can help you with that: Right there. Begin right there, where you are, right now. Do something. Save your money for an exposure camp. Contact a club's GM or coach (find them!). Send your video to an agent or team. Use your brain and get creative, we're *hustling*, remember? Do not insult your own intelligence by saying you "can't find any information" on your goal.

So you want to play pro sports, one of the hardest jobs to acquire in the world — and you "can't find" anything? *Are you kidding me?* I can't take you seriously. You're online and you found this. Which means you know what Google is and what it does. *Are you that lazy?* Be honest. Yes? Then let me save you some time: Forget basketball. Apply for a job at McDonald's — it's easy, safe, and they'll tell you exactly what to do — how to do the work, what to wear to work, when to eat lunch, and when to go home. It's predictable and you even get free "food".

I wrote this post because, no matter how much I have written, I keep getting the same damn messages from players who come to me as if I'm the hoops Wizard of Oz who will answer all their basketball-life's questions with godly wisdom — I do actually do that, but not the type of wisdom many unsatisfied emailers receive. I tell them the equivalent of what you are reading right now and people get mad at me for telling them to take control of their situations.

Why won't you help me??!!

I don't know you or your situation — don't bother sharing your life's story in an email. Not because I don't care, but because I'm not interested in taking the reins to your life. My goal — when I write these things, when I make those motivational videos — is to influence you into *empowering yourself*. That's the endgame. That's how you make an impact. That's how you can make a name for yourself, in sports any anything else.

I think I've said enough. Waiting for the next email.

#WOYG

How To Get Overseas Decision-Makers To Open (And Reply To) Your Emails

When I was grinding to get my overseas basketball career started and/or keep it going, I sent so many emails just trying start a conversation with someone, anyone, form team that could possibly sign me to a contract. In getting my deal in Montenegro in 2007, I sent over 750 emails between September and December alone. The negotiations and finalizing emails (i.e., the time between the first reply I received form my eventual team and our agreement and flight ticket being sent to me) took about 10 messages in total.

I know that the grind continues for players who are coming up these days. This post will cover a few guidelines for how you can make your messages stand out, get read and replied to, and even who to reach decision makers in other ways with the new tools of engagement available to us.

For Emails

Make Your Headline Stand Out. You're not the only player sending them. If you have the idea, guess how many others have the same idea? Write a subject line that would make you want to open it. I tried many different headlines, one way that got a few responses was by listing my measurements along with my name (Dre Baldwin 6'4" 185 PG/SG, for example).

Sell Yourself! Your subject line gets your email opened. Now, give them some substance. Who are you, were are you from, how old are you, what are your measurements (don't lie)? Where have you played? No need to be too specific with your history in the first message with stats and such -- just say where you have played. If they want stats, they'll ask.

Keep Your First Message Simple And Pithy. Get to the point and be clear about what you're writing for - remember that the person on the other end doesn't know you and has no need for too many formalities. Grabbing their attention is pivotal though -- transfer some enthusiasm in your text (which means using exclamation points!) Make it clear what your aim is in your first sentence so the person reading it knows what it is you want, and they can read with that in mind.

Include A Video. If you don't have one, stop sending emails and get one. Don't have any game film to make a highlight from, and no games on your schedule? Ok, go to the gym and film yourself. As a decision-maker, I need to see something, anything, that tells me that you can play other than your words. Anyone can make any claim in an email -- show me proof of what you're saying. Especially at this point in our world of easy digital video -- without it, your chances of getting a reply are quite slim.

Give Them A Call To Action. Know what you want to happen next. What do you want to the reader to do with your email? Do you want them to reply? Do you want them to offer you a contract based on your email? Do you want to set up a Skype call?

Beyond Email

The great thing now is that you can reach teams, agents and coaches through other networks, like social media.

However You Reach Out, Don't Be A Pest. If you don't get a reply, sending the same message over and over again will not get the elusive response -- it will get you sent to a spam folder (or blocked on Facebook).

Have Some Life To Your Profile. If you utilize LinkedIn or Facebook or Twitter, don't start contacting coaches from a barren, just-made-it-yesterday profile. Fill in all the "About" info, interact with people outside of your sales pitches, be human being. People will notice this.

When Talking, Less Is More. Remember that you are talking to people who are from different countries and cultures than you are. Don't get too familiar in your communication until they show you it's OK to do so. When someone asks you a question, answer it and shut up.

Always Leave The Ball In Their Court with a question or test-close (what would you need from me to bring me onto your club? Do you see how a player of my abilities could help your team?). Don't give more information than you're asked for. At the same time, they are people -- don't be a damn robot. Have a personality but don't get too friendly.

Outside of actually meeting the decision makers face to face at camps and tryouts, emailing is a free, easy way to make headway with the people who could possibly put you where you want to be. But know up front that the response rate is generally low and you're swimming in a crowded pond. But, it can work. Pay attention to the results you're getting and don't be too stubborn to change up your strategies if it's not working. Be persistent and it just might work.

How Good Do You Have To Be?

People ask me this question as if there is some measure I can give them. There isn't, but I do have some guidelines that could help you gage if you're up to par:

You Must Be Disciplined. Discipline Is A Skill. There are practices — lots of practices — and often many more practices than games (I have experienced as much as a 10:1 ratio, practicing twice per day Monday-Friday and having one game per week on Saturday). You have to show up and show out, especially since you are one of a few — and maybe the only — foreign guy there: You are held to a different standard. Everyone is watching you, every day. You cannot be late. You can't coast, even when everyone else is.

Shit Ain't Fair. Can You Perform Through It? Refs have no incentive to give you calls; actually it's quite the opposite. You're an American, you're *supposed* to score through that obvious uncalled foul (especially if you're the most athletic guy on the floor — don't expect whistles unless there's an egregious play). You're an American, you're *supposed* to score on that guy easily, even as he holds you every time you move (see next point). You're an American, this freezing cold, dusty gym shouldn't stop you from dominating the game/practice (what a coach told me — through my teammate translator — in practice one day in Montenegro).

Everything Should Be — Or Appear To Be — Easier For You Than Everyone Else. An agent I was dealing with in Germany brought me to practice with some team. One part of practice was a 1-on-1 drill and I found myself matched up with this long and lanky 19-year-old German kid. In 5 attempts on offense and defense, I scored and every time and the German kid scored zero. The floor was dusty as fuck though, and I couldn't make hard cuts, so I used a lot of basic stuff to score — footwork, posting, shot fakes, etc. Later that night, said agent and his assistant said to me, 'yeah you scored, but it was too hard for you. You have to score on him easily, like with one dribble.' This way of thinking was and is complete bullshit, but that's the way they look at Americans in many places.

You'd Better Dominate. And Make Everyone Else Perform Better. If You Do Only One Or The Other, Something's Wrong With You. I came to a team once in the middle of the season, replacing a point guard who was averaging 30 points per game. He was doing great and the team was OK, but the complaint from management was that the replaced player wasn't helping the improvement of any of the young guys (read: Local players from that country who represent the future of the country/ organization); he was just out for himself. I also played on a team where I played more of the all-around role — passing up scoring opportunities to set up other guys, focusing on defense and rebounding — and was told, in no uncertain terms, that I'd better put some points on the board if I planned on sticking around in that league, or any other league for that matter, as an American 2-guard. You are Superman. Every day. And as soon as you slip up, they'll start looking for a new Clark Kent.

You Will Be Battling Other Americans For Your Job, Check, And Career. Some people in the USA think that if they go play overseas it'll be easy pickings, going up against some soft European ballplayer. They don't get that many times you won't be facing Euros at all — your matchup is that one American guy the other team has. All game. You guard him, he guards you. It'll be just like you're back in the states, except your job is on the line. And your future jobs, too, as everyone in that league is watching that matchup. You ready to complete against another guy who is playing for his family's food?

Many Clubs' Training Methods Are 20 Years Behind The USA's. Deal With It. Some teams don't know what a dynamic warmup is. A foam roller? Good luck. With all the information we have these days, we know that the 170 pound, 5'9" point guard and the 7-foot, 285 pound center should not be doing the same weightlifting routine. But I have been on clubs where the lifting program was one-size-fits-all, and you'd better do it. Think you're going to explain to the coach how you don't like doing the bench press or triceps extensions because it'll mess up your shot? How you don't squat because it isn't good for your knees in-season? How will you do that, when you're supposed to be the shining example for the rest of the team? How, when the coach or trainer doesn't even speak fluent English? You're asking out of weight room work when everyone else is doing it? *You, the American?* No chance.

If You Are Still Asking "How Good You Need To Be To Play Pro Ball", You Aren't Good Enough. Yet. Change Your Thinking. This is a plain and simple fact. See that perfect 10 woman at the other end of the bar? If you have to ask yourself, for even a second, if you're in her league to go approach her, you aren't. Period. If you're not sure you're good enough to play basketball for money, you ain't there yet.

The good news is, you don't have to stay that way. You can make the conscious decision to step your game — your *mental* game — up. There is not much of a support system when you're in some foreign country and can't speak the language and have nothing familiar around you and everyone is expecting everything from you. They're expecting support from *you*. Understand? You're the strong one. You're the leader. You're the example-setter. This is called mental fortitude. Questioning yourself and your abilities is the exact opposite of mental fortitude. You need to get yourself some, and never run out of it, if you're going to make a profession out of this.

What Makes A "Professional"?

There are more players walking around the gyms and playgrounds of the world who feel they could play pro ball than there are available roster spots. This means, you need to have qualities that separate you from the rest. If you think your differentiating skill is that you can score more points than the next guy, good luck. EVERY player thinks he/she can score 30. And even if you do, that doesn't make you unique. We've all had our stat-sheet moments — and every player holding down the job you want has, too. So try again in deciding what makes you different.

Being a professional has nothing to do with what team you're on (or if you're even *on a team*) or how much money you have/make or how many points you had in your last game. The following qualities are what makes a pro, a pro. These apply to any aspect of life, as there are professional dog trainers, auto mechanics, and music producers. These traits are all 100% under your control and you can assume all of them, on purpose, right now.

Showing Up Every Day, And People Knowing They Can Count On You To Show Up. There are lots of distractions out there for athletes. Resting on our laurels, chasing our sexual desires, hanging with our non-athlete friends, easier and less physically taxing ways to make a living. I was in the gym working out some years ago and played this kid one-on-one. We talked after and he told me he really wanted to play overseas or college ball, since he hadn't played since high school. Sizing him up — he was far from pro-ready but he had some skill to build on — I figured he would at least be useful as a practice dummy, so I told him to come to the gym every day and he could work out with me.

He lasted about three weeks and I haven't seen nor heard from him since. I doubt he made it to college or pro ball.

Showing Up Alone Is A Skill. If you make a point of just showing up, on time, every time, you'll outlast 90% of your competition.

Besides Your Family, Career Is First In Line. Everything you do should be done with business considered first. Yo *could* go out Friday night, but how will you be able to get up for Saturday's gym session? You *could* give in to peer pressure and take that shot of Patron, but think about how you'll feel the next afternoon when your trainer or workout partner is pushing you past fatigue. Will that patron help or hurt you? Spend the evening walking the mall, or staying off your feet to rest your feet and legs? If you choose to put the pursuit of pussy or "turning up" in the club with your friends ahead of your business, just know that *you* chose to do so, no one else.

Understanding That It Is Not Just About Talent (Unless You Are In The Top .05%). The top .05% — that's one-half of one percent, for this of you who hate reading decimals in percentages, like me — are the ones who have been star players their entire lives, were stars in high school, (went straight to the NBA or) high-D1 scholarship, first round draft pick (leaving school early) regardless of their college production, and will always be given a chance to play somewhere because their amazing talent is too much to risk missing out on.

Does all of this description sound like your basketball career thus far? No? That's Ok, it's not mine either. This just means that talent alone will not save you. You have a nasty crossover? You can dunk with two hands off the vertical? An open jumpshot is a layup to you? Cool. Me too. And 10,000 other players, too. If you didn't leave college early to enter the NBA Draft, your talent is not one-of-a-kind, which means you are replaceable. There is another player out there, who can do everything you can do, who wants your job. Are your current actions making it easier or harder for her to take that job from you?

Anyone Can Get Lucky Once. Can You Build On It? Getting one contract and playing for one team is great: Now your foot is in the door. You *should* feel good. Now what will you do — kick your feet up and relax, or assume the actions of your new position? Reaching a higher level means you need to work and focus *more*, not less. Signing a contract makes you a target for all those players who are still in the place you just left. They want what you have. How will you defend it?

Vanilla Ice made one great record. Ever see those half court shots at halftime of NBA games? It's great when someone makes one. Think they could make it twice?

I always feel that a person has to do something at least twice to prove it wasn't a fluke. Prove it wasn't luck by doing it again.

Getting Paid Does Not Make You A Pro. Getting The Job Done Every Day, No What Your Emotions Are Saying, Is What Makes You A Pro. This is what Cus D'Amato (Mike Tyson's trainer, and the man who taught Mike boxing) told Mike Tyson before a fight while Cus lay on his deathbed. Mike went out and won his fight, because that what a professional does: Block out all distractions, put emotions on mute, and go to work.

If you're on the sideline right now, you can "go pro" by changing your mindset. Pro is not about your physical location, material possessions, or even who knows your name. Pro is how you treat your craft. Are you consistent? Do you treat your work like a business (even when there is no money coming in)? Do you consider the effect that your daily actions have on your pro-ness? If you want to be something or someone, start acting like you already are.

Can Someone Go Pro From A Small School?

Short Answer: Yes. I've done it.

Practical/Reasonable Answer: Probably not. But if you think being practical or reasonable (or thinking in this way) is going to get you from a Division III college campus gym to a professional basketball contract, you are in the wrong book.

If you didn't know, I played at a NCAA Division 3 (also referred to as D3 or DIII or NCAA3) college. D3 schools do not offer athletic scholarships and, as you can probably surmise, are the bottom of the totem pole in terms of talent and exposure and pro players produced. These are realities of D3 sports.

Your personal realities, however, are 100% your decision.

Let's start from the top.

When I was a junior in high school and had my first tastes of basketball success, I decided where my life was going: I was going to play basketball for a living. I had no idea where I was going to college yet or how I'd get on the basketball team at said school (since I was not even on my high school varsity roster as a junior), but the decision had been made. That decision played more of a role in everything that has happened since then than anything else — my ability to dunk, a jumpshot, any camps I played at, a crossover move.

If you are at a D3 school and want to play ball professionally, there may not be many people who will be able to relate to your ambitions; some may even discourage you (I had no shortage of this). You are entering the professional world, which means you are fully responsible for your actions and fully responsible for the results, and just the same for the lack of either.

Here are some pieces of information that will make things clear for you.

Whether You *Can* Play At Any Level Is Like Having Sex With A Girl: If You Have To Ask, The Answer Is Probably "No." Do you believe you? Not many people are going to jump on your bandwagon until you turn the damn key and start driving it.

Players ask me dumb ass question sometimes. Such as, "How good do I have to be to _____ (play some level of basketball)?" Are levels of basketball "goodness" definable by words? Not in my estimation. What do you expect me to tell you? You need to be 85% of Lebron-Level? Just slightly worse than Jeremy Lin?

At this point in my life/career, the question concerning any player is simple.
Can you play?

I don't care about your assessment of your skills, your physical measurements, or your stats. It's a yes or no question. Nothing to add. No qualifications. Yes or No. This is something you need to answer for yourself, not to me.

Many NCAA D3 Players Have No Ideas Or Aspirations Of Playing Basketball Beyond College. That Doesn't Mean You Have To Be One Of Them. I know this first hand. Many of my college teammates looked at D1 players as some sort of demigods whom they could not see or touch, only talk about. Many of my teammates saw themselves as basketball minions who just wanted to play their years at our D3 school then put the basketball down forever, completely satisfied with a career that ended in obscurity at a school that garnered no recognition nor respect.

Just that very thought made me sick.

Most people are reasonable. They stay in their place, don't overstep imaginary boundaries, are happy with whatever they receive, and want everyone around them to behave the same way. And since this is their reality, they have no choice but to advise you to have the same reality — they don't know any other way of thinking. It is very important that you understand this. Re-read the previous two sentences again. Hell, copy+paste them to some location where you'll see them daily if you need to.

You have to make the decision on what you are going to be about, what you are going to do. Coming from an environment where you may be the only one thinking how you are thinking, your resolve must be twice as strong.

People Who Don't Know You And Have Never Seen You Play Will Judge Your By Your Resume. Your Only Goal Needs To Be To Have Them See You On The Court. *Then* **Things Can Change.** At the end of my junior year of college I was soon to be home in Philadelphia and I remembered what my since-fired sophomore year coach had told me: If you haven't gotten destroyed on the court (or crossed over badly or dunked on), that's because you ain't playing against anyone who can play.

With that in mind, I made a call to the organizer of the Del-Val Pro-Am held at Drexel University in Philly. He asked the usual questions — are you in/ from the area, where do you play, etc. I told him the D3 school I was at and he was instantly not-so-interested in me. He told me I could come down to Drexel when the games started and he would see what he could do (which did not sound like much).

Long story short, my car was out of commission by the time I got home for the summer so I missed out, but the point of all this is simple:

As soon as you leave that D3 campus where you're The (Wo)Man because you're one of only 12 on campus with a basketball team uniform, you go back to being Nobody. You have to prove yourself all over again, and your resume of being a D3 player won't do much for you. Your goal at this point is to get yourself on the court, where everything is equal, and you can make your point that way. Once you step on a court, there are no stats or trophies or pedigrees or any of that other shit. It's just a court, the ball and the players. On the court, you are the player your performance says you are. This is one reason why players attend exposure camps: To show that they can play on a level which their previous experience and results does not say they can.

So in conclusion, D3 player: Yes, you can play professional/overseas basketball coming from where you're coming from. Let this be the last time you have to look outside of yourself for the answer to that question.

How I Got My First Overseas Contract

(Short Version; the longer story will be in my book #SignDreBaldwin — no release date yet as I'm still writing it)

I knew where I was going with my life as my senior year of college wound down: Basketball was my future. There was no alternative idea, though I was prepared to do the things necessary to survive until I got into my career.

1. I attended a pro exposure camp.
2. I got my video from said camp.
3. I put the scouting report from the camp, along with my video, together into a player resume/profile.
4. I reached out to agents with my profile to see if any were interested. One guy was.
5. I was working full time during this period.
6. I worked on my game with a schedule, like it was a second job.
7. I applied for a passport months ahead of time.
8. I kept in touch with my agent regularly.
9. I signed.

Choosing The Right Pro Basketball Exposure Camp

If you attend a big school (read: NCAA Division 1), professional clubs will seek *you* out because of where you played. For the rest of us — NCAA 2 & 3, junior colleges, NAIA, no college basketball experience — creating a career in basketball ain't easy.

Notice I said "creating," not "getting." You will have to take proactive steps, yourself, to make shit happen. I talked about this in the opening chapter; what you're reading now addresses the "Show Your Game" and "Network" directives: Pro Exposure Camps and Combines.

I have been to at least 10 over the last 8 years — I'd estimate that 4 or 5 were worth it — and I hope some of you can learn from my experiences and save yourself a lot of time, money and headaches.

Three Things You Can Gain From A Camp. Yes, attending a camp, especially in a place you otherwise wouldn't have been, can be a great experience. You'll meet other players and people, and take lots of pictures. Speaking strictly form a business standpoint — and this is a business, you will soon find out — there are three clear objectives: 1) Signing a contract to play for a team; you know by the time you leave the camp that you'll be playing for a certain club when the time comes, and it's on paper. 2) Making contact with an agent or team manager or player, who can get you closer to #1. 3) Having video/scouting report from the camp that can get you closer to #1 and/or #2. Otherwise, why go?

Do Your Research And Shop Around. Camps cost money — most charge anywhere from $150-500 for the camp fee alone, aside from your travel, lodging and food costs (some will include — maybe partially — such things). Thusly, know *exactly* what you're getting when you spend your money. You are making an investment in your potential career with money you worked hard for — accept no bullshit. These camps are not doing you a favor by having you attend. Let me repeat this very important point:

THESE CAMPS ARE NOT DOING YOU A FAVOR BY HAVING YOU ATTEND. Pro camps are money-making enterprises for the organizers. Don't let them fool you. Every player that signs up and shows up is profit for them. If you're at least a competent player while sharing the floor with pros, they want you there.

If you sense a camp isn't all it seems, move on to the next one. If a camp couldn't take the time to create a professional — looking website, why would they take time to worry about your situation, after they've got your money? They won't. I've learned this the hard way so you don't have to.

Nowadays there are hundreds of camps every summer — here's one resource — you don't have to fall over yourself to try getting into any one in particular. If a certain camp has a lot of guys who got signed before, those same guys may be there again, getting minutes, shots, and attention from the decision makers. I know what your pride is telling you as a response to that sentence — you want to compete with those guys and prove you are just as good, right? Nothing wrong with that. Just know that the more you are being paid attention to, the better your chances. Choose wisely.

Reach Out To Last Year's Participants. On a camp's website or Facebook page, there will usually be a list of players from the previous year who did well there or signed contracts. Reach out to those guys — everyone is on Facebook. There's Twitter, email, hell, just Google people. Ask them about the camp — how it was, did the camp deliver everything it claimed? Would you go again? Worst-case scenario, you get no response. Best-case, you get useful, unfiltered, from-the-source information from someone who lived it. Talk to a few and you'll get a good idea of what you're getting into.

Contact The People In Charge. Like I said, a camp is a business for the people running them — businesses, to stay profitable, better show respect to their customers (you). If a combine organizer won't return your email or call in a timely fashion (or throws out an "I'm so busy" excuse), that's a red flag. If an organizer gets annoyed with you for asking too many questions, is evasive with information/details, or seems to just be telling you what you want to hear to get you to shut up and pay your non-refundable entry fee — red flags.

Organizers should be willing and able to answer every question, even offering to speak with you via telephone/Skype, etc., if you're trying to give them your money. Don't buy any "busy" excuses — if a person puts a camp together, yes, they're busy — figuring ways to maximize profit on their business venture. I attended a camp of an agent that, at the time, had a stable of around 60 players, 85% of them signed and playing (this is the kind of camp that, in hindsight, I wouldn't have attended — I wasn't a client of his and his camp was designed to showcase his players. But that's not my point here). I showed interest in his camp, and he took every measure to make sure I got there and was situated properly — even getting on the phone with me to discuss details, and meeting me at my hotel the night before the camp to introduce himself. Another camp I attended, the organizer picked everyone up from the airport himself, in his car. You should expect the same.

All That Glitters Ain't Gold. A common ploy camps use in advertising is claiming that a certain number or percentage of previous attendants signed contracts. I won't even go as far as advising you to avoid such camps — there wouldn't be much left if you did — but if a camp makes such a claim, it should be displaying names, photos and 'team signed with' out there next to their claims. Sometimes a player attends a camp and later signs with a pro team, but the signing had nothing to do with his attendance/performance at said camp. The camp, however, will use that players' signing as credibility for their camp. There is a simple way to at least try to get to the bottom if this — when you contact some of the players, ask them if the camp was directly related to his signing.

Some of the people that are running Winning Ways were previously affiliated with InfoSport, but they were not owners of InfoSport. As the owner of the company, I chose to no longer work in the basketball industry, for the EXACT reasons that you outline in your video. There are too many people taking advantage of unsuspecting players, and not delivering on the services they claim to offer.

InfoSportSoccer   1 week ago

Winning Ways is NOT the same company as InfoSport. InfoSport no longer works in the basketball industry as of 2008, because we feel that too many companies are in the basketball business misleading players and simply running events such as this for the benefit of making money. The overwhelming majority of players listed on the Winning Ways web site, that played professionally, were attendees of an InfoSport combine, NOT a Winning Ways camp. There is a very big difference.

InfoSportSoccer   1 week ago

[A response from the owner of a company whose camp I attended in 2005.]

Tilt The Odds In Your Favor. The fewer players attending the camp you attend, the more attention your abilities will get. The coaches and scouts that attend camps to find talent are human — they can only take in so much at a time. I wouldn't remember much about each of 150 individual players from watching them over two days — I may just fixate on the 6'-10" big man or the guard who made his first two shots when I walked into the gym. Most camps these days will advertise that all games are on film for talent evaluators to review. But think about it: The purpose of going to a camp is to be seen, and possibly be approached by, a person who can change your future. If a team is looking to sign a player, a person with the power to do so will be present at your camp, looking. If a team is going to sign you off of a video they watched, they can do that from home.

A camp shouldn't have more than 8 players per team for full court games. If you get placed on a team where you won't be able to play your position, see what can be done to get you on a different team. Find camps that have scheduled practice or drill sessions on-court aside from the full court games — practices, drills, group/position-specific workouts, etc. This is the best way for any player to get comfortable and display his strengths.

Get The Video. By the time of this writing, this should go without saying, but a lot of camps are still not getting this essential point right. Any camp that doesn't offer video to participants, *to take with you on the spot* (can be a DVD, media file emailed to you, video transferred to a USB stick of yours — have one available), is worthless. Get your video while you're there. If they don't make it clear that you can get video before you leave — red flag. Ask around, and ask the camps about the video — almost every camp will make the claim, and many will not come through as promised.

Where Are The Decision Makers? All camps will use the attendance of pro coaches/managers/ scouts/agents to lure you in, and they will try to have as many as possible there. So, that camp should have names, titles and photos of the decision makers coming, before you sign up. That way they can't lie later on (screen-capture what they post), and you can cross-reference what you see when you get there, with what the camp advertised. If a camp is evasive about specifics on who's coming to the camp, there's a 98.4% chance they are overselling themselves to get your money — probably the most oft-used selling tool for professional basketball combines. Red flag.

Go Abroad If You Can. I'm an American basketball player, and any other American reading this who's been to a few camps can attest: American players play very selfishly at camps. One or two guys make a couple shots early, and never stop shooting. I've been to all types of camps — league-run, agent-run, company-run — it's the same wherever you go. Players in other countries don't play with the same 'get-yours' mentality that we have. Passing, screen-setting, and making the extra pass are normal to them.

Foreign coaches expect the same, and frown on selfish play. You have a better chance of getting good, clean offensive opportunities (willing passers, plays being run, playing on a team with legitimate 'big men') in a European camp. Many American combines cut corners (and costs) when it comes to coaching. They bring in some local guys, or people from their organizations, to coach a team (or a coach who is trying to get a job, just like you — they spend more time trying to prove themselves than making sure every player's abilities are maximized). Most of them aren't coaches by trade. Many of them — from my experience — run things more like fans than coaches.

The European camps I've been to bring in real-life professional basketball coaches, who coach the teams you want to sign and play for. This is the way it should be done. Imagine a coach in Country X watching your film from some American camp in which there are no plays being run, no defense, everyone is a guard, and everyone is trying to score 30 points — you're scoring a bunch of points. What is it worth?

Be Wary Of Roll-The-Ball-Out Camps. This refers to camps at which all you do is play games right off the bat — no drills, no practices. I warn you to be wary because you never know what the situation will be. You may be a guard forced to play power forward, a point guard that never gets to handle the ball. At least with camps that have scheduled drill and practice sessions, you can get loose, display your strengths, and let the decision makers & coaches get familiar with you. A 6'7" point guard who attends a roll-the-ball-out camp may find himself playing center if there's no practice/workout session for him to establish his position and what he can do. And that would suck.

Step Back And Take A Deep Breath. Some players will have agents who cover the costs for them to attend camps, covering the player's travel expenses as you try to get your career off the ground. Personally, I have never been in that situation — I've spent my own money to get where I went. Sometimes, money I earned while thinking about how great it would be to earn money from basketball, instead of (fill in full-time/9-to-5 job I *really* didn't want to be at).

If you're looking for a camp to attend, that means you're a serious player who is passionate about wanting to make a living from this game. So when you're deciding on a camp, detach yourself from your emotions and make a rational, measured decision — if you were watching another person whom you didn't know, who's about to do what you're about to do, what would you think? Is this person being smart? Is she only thinking about the greatest possible outcome, ignoring all the possible pitfalls and obvious holes in her plan?

Take a moment, an entire day if you can, to clear your head and think hard about what you're investing in before pulling the trigger. Emotions are bad decision-makers.

At Camp: Communicate With The Coaches. Let them know what position you play and/or if you're willing to play a different position due to team personnel. Speak up if you aren't playing enough — you paid for the chance to be seen! From my experience, about half the coaches at camps are very clear and upfront about playing time and how things will be done, and they stick to it. The other half "coach to win," and leave players on the bench. Know who you're dealing with and get what you paid for. Before you know it, the camp will be over. Speak up for yourself.

On The Court: Stay In Your Lane. If you don't shoot threes, you don't have to shoot a three just because the ball finds you behind the arc. It is very easy to see when a player is trying to do more than he's capable of, and it makes that player look bad. It only takes one dumb decision to kill your chances for that particular audience. At one camp I attended, I violated this rule by forcing up a bad — and badly missed — shot. I knew, the very moment after that shot, that I wouldn't be getting a call from any coach or agent in that gym.

For Your Career: Who You Know Will Get You In The Door. What You Can Do Will Keep You In The Building. When you do sign a contract, congratulations. Now you have to earn it and keep it. I know too many players who played in one place, off of one deal, and their careers ended when that season did.

Overseas contracts aren't like the NBA, they're more like the NFL – the team can cut you at any moment, for any reason, and owes you nothing. Bad game? Couple of sluggish days of training (practice)? You could be gone just as soon as you got there. I know players that got released from contracts after one game with their new team. I know players who were released before even playing in a game; you are being evaluated even in practice. So be prepared for the long haul — we're talking about a career here.

Attend Exposure Camps & Reaching Out To Agents/Teams While Still In School

Sometimes players ask me about attending professional exposure camps for overseas basketball, or reaching out to agents or professional teams while they still have college basketball eligibly remaining. *Is it a good idea to go to a camp even though I have years of college ball yet?*

Here's how you can decide if that's for you, along with information you really should know.

- The only reason you should be attending a pro exposure camp is if you are ready to leave school and take an offer you may receive because of your performance at said camp. The international basketball market is not the NBA -- there is no "radar" or Draft Board where teams are following you and waiting for you to finish school just so they can swoop in and sign you.

The NBA is every player's first option; overseas is the second option. So overseas team can only grab a player whose NBA/D-League options aren't sufficient. Thusly, team don't even care about you until you express that you care about them (for the most part -- some high-level players from top-tier D1 programs will receive offers that they must weigh against NBA opportunities).

Attending a camp when you have no intentions of leaving school yet -- meaning you have your senior year ahead of you and you plan on competing school -- is a waste of time and money; even if you go there and average 50 points, you'll have to go prove yourself all over again the next year (teams will want to know if you're still as good as you used to be if that were to happen), spending your money all over again, too.

- **Discussing contracts with agents and/or professional teams while you are playing NCAA basketball could forfeit your eligibility.** If you're in college, you know that the NCAA is not a governing body to play games with (no pun intended). If you're playing college ball, you are an amateur. Talking to professionals in your sport such as team managers and agents could cause the NCAA to deem you a professional, thus ruling you ineligible to play (and even if you're wrongly accused, you have seen how long the NCAA takes to clear things up so you can pay again).

In short: Don't be stupid. An athlete talking to an agent is a red flag that can kill your college career just like that. If you're a basketball player on a college campus, you're easy to spot in a crowd, and people you have never even noticed know exactly who you are and know how to get you in trouble. Be smart.

What I Know About Exposure Camps

The Cheaper The Camp, (Usually) The Less Credible It Is (exception: local D-League camps, which I will get to below). You get what you pay for. A camp that is worth it and that is really bringing in the scouts they advertise will charge higher entry fees because they know they're worth it.

Cheaper Camps = More Participants. $100-$150 is a small amount to bet on a chance you could make a professional basketball team (or even have a cool story about how you tried out). Cheap camps will attract lots of players, including many that know they could not cut it on a pro team. If it seems like easy money to you, a bunch of other players are seeing the same thing. Beware.The NBA D-League has a national camp in a few big cities, then each club has their own tryouts in several cities each year which will run you $100-200 to try out and can be either one or two days.

I know players who have attended local D-League camps which had 80 or more attendees for a one-day tryout (me being one of them). I know players who've attended camps that didn't have enough players to go 5-on-5. One thing for sure about the D-League local tryouts is that the team can run it in any manner they choose and often make it up as they go along depending on who's there (and how many) and the whims of the person in charge (usually the team's head coach). The D-League is a great opportunity, we know. Be careful with your money, however, when chasing that pot of gold. Everyone knows that paying $150 for the outside chance they could make the D-League is a bet worth taking. The more bettors there are, the lower your odds of winning.

Camps Run By Agencies Cater To Their Clients First, Non-Clients Second. By this I mean, making sure you are with a team/coach/situation that displays you in your best light. The agency is financially invested (meaning, money: The #1 motivation for most of the moves made in the basketball business) in seeing you do well in the case that you're their client. If you are there, but not a client of the agency, what incentive do they have to help you look good? If another player with a similar resume and physical profile is signed with them, that agency would rather *him* get the contract than you get it. Simple logic. I have been to several agency-run camps and seen this in action.

Men Lie, Women Lie, Money Does Not. This is a dirty-ass game and there are a lot of people in it for the fast buck who could not give less of a damn about basketball, nonetheless your career. If you see a flyer for a camp (ranging $100-200) run by a person/company you've never heard of, do your due diligence and Google them/him/her. If this entity really has sent players overseas, it will be very clear whom and when and where. Can't find it? That's for good reason.

Beware "We're Sending/Streaming This Video To Coaches/Teams In _____ (Insert Random Country Or Countries)." One day in 9th grade we had a substitute teacher. The sub had attended Central High in Philly; we were students at E&S High. Both schools are high-ranking academically, and the substitute teacher got into a debate with students about which school was better.

We boasted our 100% college acceptance rate and the substitute teacher shot that down by informing us of the following: the Community College of

Philadelphia sent acceptance letters to every student at schools like ours (and his), without us even applying.

That said, technically, I could tell you that if you send me a video of yourself playing that I'm sending it to 10 teams overseas and not, technically, be lying. I could send an email or post the video on my website and say I made it available to clubs in Japan and Australia and that's the truth... It's also available to President Obama if he happens to stumble across my site. If an agent or company claims to have contacts in certain places, they should have players playing there or have those contacts sitting in the bleachers watching you (which should be clear before you register). Be discerning.

Camps Held In Las Vegas in July Have The Highest "Exposure" Possibilities Among US Camps — And The Fiercest Competition. Camps held at this time of year in Vegas are at the same time as the NBA Summer League, which draws the highest-level decision-makers in the business of basketball. Every other camp will advertise this proximity — and many times, thats all it is: Proximity

— as one of their virtues. Knowing this, know that the competition at these camps will be the highest — the best players looking for the same jobs you're looking for, the highest volume of players. At the same time, these camps will also have the most scouts/agents/coaches in attendance watching you.

The Best Camps for Me, In My Experience, Were Held In Europe. Several reasons why: 1) More scouts and coaches will show up since it is closer for them, and travel within European countries is relatively cheap. 2) There will be fewer players in general (and fewer Americans). We Americans are dreamers — when we couldn't break 15 points in a rec league, we'll still pony up $150 to try out for the D-League. Europeans, in my experience, tend to have a more practical worldview — by age 21, they know if basketball is their future or if it isn't. Meaning, there won't be so many of them trying out at some camp because they're seeking a cheap thrill. In US camps, this is prevalent. 3) The foreign scouts can watch you perform under game conditions (officiating, coaching, style of play) similar to the ones you'd play under if you were to be signed by them. These European camps also cost much more — usually around $300-450 and up just to register for the camp (usually includes the double-room hotel stay, 1-2 meals per day, camp uniform) — and you cover your own travel costs. You are looking at an investment of around $2,000 when everything is factored in. I have been to a few European-based pro camps and the experiences alone made them worth it.

All Of This Stated, One Great Stretch Of Play Can Change Your Future. That's all it takes. You ready?

Overseas Basketball And Money: What You Should Know

How much would I get paid playing overseas?
What's the average overseas salary?
How much did YOU get paid playing overseas?
Do I need an agent?

A lot of people — players and otherwise — seem to want to know the answer to these one. I will do my best to clear things up.

The differences between playing overseas and the NBA — where pay is concerned — are 1) NBA salaries are public record, overseas salaries are not, and 2) The NBA has a salary scale. With international teams, some clubs will publish their total roster budget, but not a list of what each player is receiving (which could lead to obvious problems).

That said, there is no minimum or maximum you can make playing basketball overseas. You get what you negotiate (or, what you accept). That places your possible pay range anywhere from playing for free, to millions of dollars.

Agents are good for knowing what a team can afford to pay a player and possibly getting you more than you can get on your own. Overseas teams, when signing a player through and agent, pay the agent a fee themselves. You do not pay your agent anything when you sign a deal internationally. If an agent tells you to pay him, or that you pay him later from your overseas contract, that agent is scamming you. Run.

[NOTE: In the USA, teams do not pay agents. In this case you *would* pay your agent; the normal rate is 2-4%. Yes, two to four percent, by law, and no more. Endorsement deals are open season and lead to a larger agent percentage, somewhere in the 10-20% range.]

[Scam Alert: I know at least three people who have been scammed out of $250 by a man named John Jordan (here's his Twitter profile and his website). I know around 10 players that were intrigued by John's pitch but kept their money. Here's how John Jordan works: He contacts you about your interest in playing overseas (almost always, a player that has yet to begin their career). He tells you about his connections and experience placing players with jobs and name-drops multiple teams/countries (tugging at the emotional strings of a recent college grad who has yet to receive a passport stamp — smart sales strategy). He then tells you he charges a $250 (or something close) fee for his services, which you must pay before he goes to work for you. The money must be sent by Western Union or some other wire-transfer service. You pay, he emails with you for a short period after (with more name and place-dropping), then disappears, with your $250, while you are still without a contract.

John contacted me in 2004 before I had begun my career. We exchanged emails for several days. After continuos questioning of his technique ("Why do you insist I pay you *before* you do the work?"), John grew annoyed with me and cut off communication. In 2005, a player I'd faced in college got scammed by John Jordan. In 2006 when I was playing for the Harlem Ambassadors, a teammate admitted to falling for the scam. And from what I hear, John is still at it. John Jordan is his real name, he is a coach who runs some basketball school in North Carolina (peep the *$500 application fee* to his academy). Beware.]

Get copies of all your contracts in the native language and in English. Teams place dubious clauses in contracts that allows the club to do shady shit. Not to say you will be able to have such clauses removed (you or your agent may), but at least you'll know you're being robbed when it happens.

I negotiated my release from one club I was on and, when it was time for my last payment, $300 was missing. We — me, the head coach, the general manager, team treasurer, and a teammate who acted as translator between myself and the coach, general manager, and treasurer — were sitting in the main office of team headquarters. The coach explained that there was a clause in my contract that stipulated that the coach could fine the team for a bad game performance (our most recent game, which we had lost), and that's where my $300 went.

I demanded that they produce a copy of my signed contract and show me that specific clause, which I would have my translating teammate read to me. They, somehow, didn't have a copy in their main office. The last thing I said was, "We will sit here all damn day, until I get my money." They sent the team treasurer to the ATM.

How much money any person makes in any line of work is their business; if they choose to discuss their business that is their decision. I choose not to.

Euros are worth more than dollars. Know the exchange rates. If you head to Europe, get paid by the Euro and not the dollar. Clubs will try to pay you in dollars to save money, especially if you broker a deal on your own without an agent.

Basketball is business. When you sign overseas, you will be more on your own than you imagined. No one to call for help, and maybe not many people to even have a conversation with. You are responsible for being informed as to what's happening. There are honest people out there working in the basketball business, and there are also people who will bleed you for all they can if they sense you aren't on top of your business. Get on top of it, and stay on top of it.

Your First Exposure Camp: What To Expect and My Advice

I get asked for this advice often so I'm writing this post to direct all who ask.

Where Can You Find A Complete List Of Camps? Nowadays, nowhere. Eurobasket.com *used to* publish a full list right here — this is where I found every camp I've ever been to — but they smelled the scent of money and now charge organizations $150 USD just to *list* their camp (very bad idea by Eurobasket, losing their stronghold on being the only place to go for overseas players, just to make a few extra bucks).

Many organizations and good camps are not paying this fee — it's a snowball effect, because as each one chooses not to, the less credible Eurobasket's listings become — which makes it harder for you, the player, to find a good camp. You will have to do some more digging now to find camps. I have listed the camps I've been to here but there are more, of course. Your best bet, in my opinion, is to go by word of mouth — ask your college coach to ask around, contact former players from your school who have been overseas. If/when you do find a prospective camp, use information from the previous chapters to vet said camp. It is your money and time, after all.

This Is Still Basketball. Nothing Special. You have played plenty of basketball if you are at this stage. And you've probably tried out, successfully, for teams before. A pro camp is higher stakes, no doubt, and this is probably your first time paying to try out for a team. But it's still just basketball. Same sized ball, same rules. The hoop is still ten feet above the floor. A layup is still two points and a free throw is still one point. A foul is still a foul. On the court, you are playing the game you've always played. Nothing changes.

Show Up And Be Prepared. Simply put, be in-shape and ready to play basketball. Pro camps may be new to you, but it's still played on a basketball court with a basketball — you're plenty familiar with those. There are no special rules that get rolled out or new dimensions to the playing area or anything like that — it's basketball. You're playing basketball against other human beings. If you can play, there will be no surprises at a camp. If you can't play, you can't hide. Period.

Be Seen And Not Heard Off The Court. The first pro camp I ever attended was only two days long. On the first night, a bunch of players, being in Orlando for the first time (like I was too), wanted to explore the club scene while there, and from what I heard, they did.

It is highly unlikely that you can land a job on a pro team strictly by your conduct off the court. But you damn sure can lose a job with your conduct off the court. This is a business trip, so treat it like one. If you don't know what "business trip" means, follow this blueprint: Go to every camp function, and when the function is over, go to your hotel room and sit your ass down.

There's nothing wrong with sightseeing, but make sure it does not interfere with your camp schedule. No nightclubs, no drinking, no girl-chasing. You can do that all year at home; can you discipline yourself for three days to begin or advance your career? Is it worth it? And if you do choose to do any of that, do it out of the sight of any camp or pro team staff attending. That would be dumb.

Stand Out. What are you good at in basketball (if you cannot answer this — *why are you attending a camp*)? Do that as best you can, make people remember you. No one needs to tell you how — if you're attending a professional camp, you must feel you're good in some way, shape or form. Show people why.

Stay In Your Lane. The absolute dumbest thing you could possibly do is try to do something you're incapable of and kill your chances in one fell swoop. Do you shoot threes? No? Then don't shoot that shit. Are you an open-court ball handler? No? Then pick the damn ball up and get it to your ball handlers. One you-know-that's-not-your-game play can undo all of your hard work. Be the player you are and nothing more.

Tolerate Teammates. You will have bad teammates who simply cannot play at this level. You will have teammates who are planning to shoot every time (and will masterfully execute that plan). You'll have loudmouth teammates who have some instruction or tip for everyone, every time down the floor.

Don't let any of these teammates get to you — they won't be your teammates 7 days from now, and the coaches are watching. Focus on the task at hand and do what you came to do. Be where *you* should be on the floor. Take *your* shots. By all means, *play defense.* Your teammates were who they were before they got there. Let them be them and *focus on you.*

Working A 9-5/Full Time Job While Pursuing Your Pro Basketball Goals

As I shared in my book *Buy A Game*, I knew my future after college was in professional basketball. I had no idea how or where or when or who would be involved, but I knew that's what I was doing.

I don't work a 9-5 anymore, but during the early years of my career I juggled the working life along with doing my best to make/keep my game pro-level ready. Here I'll share some of what I did; maybe some of this will help you.

I had a job as a membership sales consultant at a gym in downtown Philly which was perfect for me, since I could use it for free to work out. Problem was, this gym's downtown location did not have a basketball court. The company had another location outside of the city, though, with a huge full court gymnasium. I was living in between the two gyms — my job was 20 minutes south, the bball court was

40 minutes north — and I had to be at work by 9 AM.

Solution: wake up at 4 in the morning, get to the basketball gym by its 5:30 opening time, work out, shower, drive straight to my job, there by 8:30. I usually had league games in the evenings — sometimes at the same gym I'd worked out in that morning — and often got caught falling asleep at my desk at work (pre-5 Hour Energy). My boss at the time actually threatened to send me home if he caught me sleeping at my desk again. My boss' boss threw me out of a district sales meeting after catching me dozing off multiple times during a quarterly district meeting (which I unsuccessfully denied, but it was quite clear I was sleeping). I later joined a gym — which I had to buy a membership for — that was much closer to my apartment, costing me a few dollars but saving me a ton of time (and maybe my job).

Something had to be sacrificed for me to get to where I wanted to be. Sleep was one sacrifice. I rarely went out and didn't party art all — my income went to living expenses and saving for whatever camp or tryout I was looking towards attending. And that is pretty much all my life was back then: Go to work, go to gym, go home. No leisure. No entertainment. Not even many dates. There was only one mission. Every single action I took was with my career in mind, even though at the time there *was* no career. If you are incapable of this simple level of discipline while building your career, you need to ask yourself if this (your current life, your hopeful life) is what you really want.

Other Random Pro Basketball FAQ

I still receive lots of questions from those who have read it (and many who haven't at the time of contact) on some things. I will cover as many of those common questions as I can here and add stuff as it comes up.

Such-and-such team/agency is interested in me and I don't know what to do. Can you give me some insight? It's great that you are making some inroads, but every situation is unique in this business. Advice on what to do with your career and why is what agents are for. And if you don't have an agent, you have decided to make your own moves and decisions. And you must live with every single one you make.

In general, a concrete offer on the table is better than a twice-as-good possible offer you're waiting on or hoping for. Especially if you do not have a resume or well-known name.

Dre, I read all your posts and watched the videos. Can you tell me anything else that is not in those to help me? No.

I have read your website and our stories are similar. I came from a small school/being cut/not respected/not playing high school or college and want to make it happen for myself. Can you help me out by linking me to some resources/ helping me get my name out there/telling me what to do? I get this type of message a lot and it annoys me. I covered this in the chapters above, namely the final bullet point: "No One Owes You A Thing."

This career choice is not cut-and-dried like becoming a doctor or managing a retail store. It's a very wide-open market with very little regulation and no pity for the weak and uneducated. If you want to be a professional, you are declaring yourself an adult. Adults make their own decisions and take 100% responsibility for what happens or doesn't happen to or for them.

Do you have any agents or scouts you can link me with? No.

I'm thinking about attending _____ (insert name) camp. I saw your write-up about it (or there is no write-up); can you tell me if I have high chances of getting a contract if I go to it? If you want to be a lawyer, you go to college, then law school, the pass the bar exam, and you are officially a lawyer. Professional basketball is not like this. There are no built-in guarantees, no matter who you are or what you do or who you know or where you go. If you're waiting for the time to be right or circumstances to be perfect before you act, good luck. Remember that pro athlete careers are very short.

I work very hard and I read all your stuff, I just need that one chance to make it! I would really appreciate your help. This is the best help anyone will ever give you, because it will serve you for the rest of your life, long after you've forgotten our conversation or your reading of this page: Help yourself. If you're not prepared to help yourself, you are not an adult, and therefore, not ready to be a professional.

Dre Baldwin is a Philadelphia native who started his professional basketball career after graduating with a Business Marketing and Management degree from Penn State Altoona in 2004. Dre started posting his training and motivational YouTube videos in 2006, creating the genre of "Basketball Workouts Online". As of early 2015, Dre has published over 4,000 videos.

Dre published his first book "Buy A Game" in 2012 and has since publish 3 others: The Mental Handbook, The Mirror Of Motivation, and The Super You.

Though no longer actively pursuing professional basketball playing opportunities, Dre still works out daily and continues to publish to his YouTube channel. He works as a professional speaker, Chair of his own Marketing & Branding company and with athletes on the mental and physical sides of their games. He resides in South Florida.

Made in the USA
Middletown, DE
03 May 2016